Edward Thomas

by VERNON SCANNELL

Published for The British Council
and the National Book League
by Longmans, Green & Co

Two shillings and sixpence net

Edward Thomas was more than a very fine nature poet. Deep and real as his love and knowledge of the countryside was, he was far too intense and particular to be identified with the Georgian poets. Vernon Scannell shows in his essay that Thomas's poetry appeals strongly to the modern sensitivity. Thomas was a seeker, and his search was no pose but a terrible reality pursued with an honesty sometimes bordering on cruelty. Self-doubting, emotionally insecure, uncertain of his own capacity to love, chafing at the limitations of life and the difficulties inherent in human relationships, Edward Thomas, with what the author calls his 'strange, haunted consciousness', was only too aware of the Other, his darker self. His poems, in C. Day Lewis's words, have 'the irresistibleness of absolute sincerity'.

Vernon Scannell was born in 1922 and is now a schoolmaster. Besides three novels he has published four volumes of poems: *Graves and Resurrections* (1948), *A Mortal Pitch* (1957), *The Masks of Love* (1960), and *A Sense of Danger* (1962).

Bibliographical Series
of Supplements to 'British Book News'
on Writers and Their Work

★

GENERAL EDITOR
Bonamy Dobrée

¶EDWARD THOMAS was born in Lambeth on 3 March 1878. He was killed at the battle of Arras on 9 April 1917.

EDWARD THOMAS

EDWARD THOMAS

by

VERNON SCANNELL

PUBLISHED FOR
THE BRITISH COUNCIL
and the NATIONAL BOOK LEAGUE
BY LONGMANS, GREEN & CO

LONGMANS, GREEN & CO LTD
48 Grosvenor Street, London, W.1.
*Associated companies, branches and representatives
throughout the world*

*Printed in Great Britain by
F. Mildner & Sons, London, E.C.1*

EDWARD THOMAS

THE poetry of Edward Thomas has been a long time in receiving the wide critical acclaim that it merits and, while there have always been a few perceptive readers to recognize the quality of his work, it is only quite recently that he has begun to be accepted more widely as a poet of singular powers, and one who has exercised a steady if fairly unobtrusive influence over some of the best of the younger poets now writing in English. It is true that F. R. Leavis, in *New Bearings in English Poetry* (1932), wrote an enthusiastic essay on Thomas, and before that Edward Garnett, Walter de la Mare, and John Middleton Murry had each recorded his admiration for the work of this frequently underrated poet, but elsewhere it was customary for critics to treat him as one of the Georgian weekend poets who had turned out one or two charming little nature pieces that were worth including in an anthology. As recently as 1950, an editor and critic of discernment, Kenneth Allott, included only two poems by Edward Thomas in the *Penguin* anthology, *Contemporary Verse*: but significantly, since then, later anthologies have given him a more generous allowance.

The reasons for such a slow growth of a proper estimation of the value of his work are not hard to find. First, and most obvious, the Georgian poets with whom his name was allied—although in fact his work never appeared in any of their publications—were regarded by later poets and critics, often unjustly, as absurd figures unworthy of serious attention. An image of the typical Georgian poet was erected and the shadow of this guy hid the real talents of some of the authentic poets who were unfortunate enough to find themselves stuck with the label. It was believed that the typical Georgian wore hairy tweeds, drank beer, played cricket and went for weekend rambles in the Home Counties and returned to his urban or suburban home to write mechanical little verses with pianola rhythms about Beauty, Love, and the holiness of Nature. Superficially Edward Thomas seemed to embody the type. He was born in a London suburb but he loved the country, was a great walker, and his prose books carried such titles as *The Woodland Life*, *The South Country* and *Four-and-twenty Blackbirds*.

Next, Edward Thomas, a professional author and literary journalist, did not write any poetry until he was thirty-six, and, when he did begin to write verse, it was at the direct suggestion of his friend, the American poet Robert Frost: circumstances which might suggest that he was not an authentic poet at all, but a skilled professional who could turn his hand to any job and produce an adequate piece of journeyman writing in almost any literary form. A casual glance at his work and Frost's might support the idea—mistaken, as I hope soon to show—that he was an imitator of the American poet. They both use the rhythms of common speech on a flexible metrical leash; their diction favours the simple words of Anglo-Saxon origin; their imagery and their themes are taken from rural life; the wind and rain blow through their poems and one meets in both of their poetic territories rustic characters, tramps, solitaries and originals. The titles of many of Thomas's poems could easily be those of poems by Frost: 'Birches', 'The Axe-Helve', 'After Apple-Picking' (Frost); 'Aspens', 'The Wasp Trap', 'Digging' (Thomas).

Another obstacle to the appreciation of Edward Thomas's true worth was the revolution in literary taste, started by T. E. Hulme, Ezra Pound and Ernest Fenollosa and modified but continued by I. A. Richards, William Empson and other critics, who have gradually, if not purposely, created a climate in which the poem which offers little or no challenge to the analytical intelligence, the poem whose primary, paraphraseable meaning surrenders itself on one or two careful readings, can scarcely be considered a serious poem at all.

Edward Thomas wrote poems about the English country-side, the weather, love and death, as did scores of poets now completely and deservedly forgotten. But Thomas did more than this. His poems allow us to see minute details of natural phenomena with microscopic clarity and these details are never seen in isolation: all is interrelated and modified in the strange, haunted consciousness of this gentle, bitter, self-doubting poet, and when we read his work we can enter his world. It is a disturbing and, at times, uncomfortable world, but it is one that it would be impossible to explore without finding much that yields both wisdom and delight.

II

Philip Edward Thomas was born in Lambeth in 1878 and he was killed at the battle of Arras on 9 April 1917. He was educated at St. Paul's School and Lincoln College, Oxford, and, while still an undergraduate, he married Helen, the daughter of James Ashcroft Noble, a literary journalist who was quick to see the promise in the young Edward Thomas's prose. Helen Thomas has written a perfunctorally fictionalized account of her meeting with and marriage to the poet in two books, *As it Was* and *World Without End*, both of which are published in one volume and together form an innocent, passionate and wholly endearing chronicle of her love for and life with her remarkable husband. Another book which gives the reader a vivid portrait of Edward Thomas and is a fascinating and moving work is *Edward Thomas: The Last Four Years*, by Eleanor Farjeon who, incidentally, appears in Helen Thomas's book as Margaret, the friend who platonically loves David (Edward Thomas). Eleanor Farjeon's book contains a generous number of Thomas's letters which reflect his intelligence, tenderness, self-contempt and habitual melancholy.

Thomas published his first book, *The Woodland Life*, when he was only nineteen and from then until July, 1915, when he joined The Artists' Rifles, he produced a stream of prose books, some of which he composed from choice but many of which were hack jobs undertaken grimly for the small sums of money they would yield. He wrote biographies, introductions, criticism, essays, stories, topographical descriptions, natural history, reviews and a rather odd work of fiction called *The Happy-go-lucky Morgans*. He wrote thirty books of prose, besides editing others.

In 1913 he met Robert Frost, who was staying in England at the time, and who was still virtually unknown. Thomas enthusiastically reviewed the American's collection of poems, *North of Boston*, and shortly after, in 1914, Frost persuaded him that he should turn the raw poetry which clearly existed in many of the prose works into actual poems. Once Thomas began, his output was prodigious, and his army service did not seem to interfere with his creative activity. It was as if a powerful barrier had been suddenly removed, and the poems that had been waiting so long for release came flowing out. But his work received almost no recognition, and editors obstinately returned the manuscripts which he submitted under the assumed name of Edward Eastaway. Apart from six poems published by his friend James Guthrie at the small Pear Tree Press in 1916, Edward Thomas saw none of his poems in print, and found few people, even privately, to recognize their value. A few months after his death in 1917 sixty-four poems were published under his correct name, and in 1918 a further seventy-one appeared. The *Collected Poems* contains a hundred and forty one.

Naturally there has been a good deal of speculation as to why Thomas did not begin earlier to write poetry, and unless the circumstances of his life and the special temper of his mind and sensibility are considered carefully the puzzle is bewildering indeed. Here was a man who, from boyhood, devoted himself with passionate enthusiasm to two chief pursuits: the exploration of literature and the exploration of nature. When he was not walking in the country studying birds, flowers, trees and wild animals he was reading his favourite poets. He was writing romantic prose when in his teens, and his verse criticism shows not merely an intuitive awareness of what poetry should be about, but an intelligent

familiarity with refinements of technique and a fine sense of
the historical continuity of English literature. He was
acutely responsive to natural beauty; he was introspective
and imaginative and fascinated by the sources and resources
of language. Yet, with all the equipment one generally
thinks of as necessary to the poet, he did not begin to write
poetry until he had reached an age when many poets have
written their best work and are either exhausted or dead.

H. Coombes suggests in *Edward Thomas* that Thomas's
chronic self-doubt and reticence, which were central to his
personality, prevented him from writing poetry until the
undoubted authority of Robert Frost gave him sanction;
also, Coombes remarks, in his capacity as a regular reviewer
of verse he would be forced to read a great deal of inferior
work and this, together with his lack of self-confidence,
would make him determined not to add to the mass of un-
readable poetastry of which there existed already a super-
abundance. Further, it seems that Thomas's work as a professional author would have left him neither the time nor
the energy to write poetry which would have done nothing
towards helping to support his wife and three children.

These explanations are fairly plausible but they leave a
major question unanswered. It seems unlikely that a poet
of Thomas's powers and of his artistic integrity would per-
mit such considerations to keep him silent. The full answer
is both simpler and more complex. The poetry of young
men, except in very special circumstances, is affirmative,
ecstatic and optimistic. When it is otherwise, it is obvious
that a dramatic persona has been adopted. Edward Thomas,
as all who knew him have testified, was from his earliest
days melancholy, self-probing and suspecting, pessimistic
and chronically conscious of the Other, the man within
who was his enemy. He was an agnostic, if not an atheist,
preoccupied with the transcience of things and with the
sense of mortality. In a way he was as much possessed by
death as Webster or Beddoes. The eye he turned upon the
spectacle of human existence was unsentimental, ironic and

profoundly sad. He valued above all other human attri-
butes the capacity for loving, but he believed that it had
been denied him. His poetic personality was not and could
not have been that of a young poet: he had to wait for
maturity before he was ready to write his poems in their
completed form, but many of them already existed like
uncut precious stones in the pages of his prose. Consciously
or unconsciously he had been writing poems all of his literary life. Consider this extract from *The Heart of England*,
published in 1906:

The chestnut blossom is raining steadily and noiselessly down upon a
path whose naked pebbles receive a mosaic of emerald light from the
interlacing boughs. At intervals, once or twice an hour, the wings of a
lonely swallow pass that way, when alone the shower stirs from its per-
pendicular fall. Cool and moist, the perfumed air flows, without lifting
the most nervous leaf or letting fall a suspended bead of the night's rain
from a honeysuckle bud. In an indefinite sky of grey, through which
one ponderous cloud billows into sight and is lost again, no sun shines:
yet there is light—I know not whence; for the brass trappings of the
horses beam so as to be extinguished in their own fire. There is no song
in wood or sky. Some one of summer's wandering voices—bullfinch
or willow wren—might be singing, but unheard, at least unrealized.
From the dead-nettle spires, with dull green leaves stained by purple
and becoming more and more purple towards the crest, which is of a
sombre uniform purple, to the elms reposing at the horizon, all things
have bowed the head, hushed, settled into a perfect sleep. Those elms
are just visible, no more. The path has no sooner emerged from one
shade than another succeeds, and so, on and on, the eye wins no broad
dominion.

Of course, some of the passage quoted above is 'fine
writing' on the late 19th century models, but the exactness
of the observation of the swallow, the brasses on the horses
and the dead-nettle spires looks forward to:

> The mill-foot water tumbled white and lit
> With tossing crystals, happier than any crowd
> Of children pouring out of school aloud.
> And in the little thickets where a sleeper
> For ever might lie lost, the nettle creeper

And garden warbler sang unceasingly;
While over them shrill shrieked in his fierce glee
The swift with wings and tail as sharp and narrow
As if the bow had flown off with the arrow.

                                                    ('Haymaking')

Referring to his own poems, Edward Thomas said in a
letter to John Freeman: 'What I have done so far have been
like quintessences of the best parts of my prose books' . . .
The truth of this is plainly demonstrated if we compare the
passage on Death and Rain from *The Icknield Way* with the
poem, 'Rain'. First, the prose extract:

The all-night rain puts out summer like a torch. In the heavy, black
rain falling straight from invisible dark sky to invisible dark earth the
heat of summer is annihilated, the splendour is dead, the summer is gone.
The midnight rain buries it away where it has buried all sound but its
own. I am alone in the dark still night, and my ear listens to the rain
piping in the gutters and roaring softly in the trees of the world. Even
so will the rain fall darkly upon the grass over the grave when my ears
can hear it no more. I have been glad of the sound of rain, and wildly
sad of it in the past; but that is all over as if it had never been; my eye
is dull and my heart beating evenly and quietly; I stir neither foot nor
hand; I shall not be quieter when I lie under the wet grass and the rain
falls, and I gone, and never can it return. There will never be any summer any more, and I am weary of everything. I stay because I am too
weak to go. I crawl on because it is easier than to stop. I put my face to
the window. There is nothing out there but the blackness and the sound
of rain. Neither when I shut my eyes can I see anything. I am alone.
Once I heard through the rain a bird's questioning watery cry—once
only and suddenly. It seemed content, and the solitary note brought up
against me the order of nature, all its beauty, exuberance, and everlast-
ingness like an accusation. I am not a part of nature. I am alone. There
is nothing else in the world but my dead heart and brain within me and
the rain without. Once there was summer, and a great heat and splendour over the earth terrified me and asked me what I could show that
was worthy of such an earth.

The prose continues, repetitive, perhaps rather too self-
indulgent in its rhetoric, but, in its own manner, darkly

evocative of the mood he wishes the reader to share with him It ends like this:

There was no good and no evil. There was life and there was death, and you chose. Now there is neither life nor death, but only the rain. Sleep as all things, past, present, and future, lie still and sleep, except the rain, the heavy, black rain falling straight through the air that was once a sea of life. That was a dream only. The truth is that the rain falls for ever and I am melting into it. Black and monotonously sounding is the midnight and solitude of the rain. In a little while or in an age—for it is all one—I shall know the full truth of the words I used to love, I knew not why, in my days of nature, in the days before the rain: 'Blessed are the dead that the rain rains on.'

The prose is one of the uncut stones which are scattered about his books, and here is the finished product, a quintessence indeed, which compresses, sharpens and focuses the diffused emotion and attitudes into a hard and polished poem: 'Rain.'

> Rain, midnight rain, nothing but the wild rain
> On this bleak hut, and solitude, and me
> Remembering again that I shall die
> And neither hear the rain nor give it thanks
> For washing me cleaner than I have been
> Since I was born into this solitude.
> Blessed are the dead that the rain rains upon:
> But here I pray that none whom once I loved
> Is dying tonight or lying still awake
> Solitary, listening to the rain,
> Either in pain or thus in sympathy
> Helpless among the living and the dead,
> Like a cold water among broken reeds,
> Myriads of broken reeds all still and stiff,
> Like me who have no love which this wild rain
> Has not dissolved except the love of death,
> If love it be for what is perfect and
> Cannot, the tempest tells me, disappoint.

III

It was writing of the quality of the passage quoted from *The Icknield Way* and the respect he felt for his friend's judgement, intellect and sensibility that made Robert Frost suggest to Edward Thomas that he should make poems, and, as we remarked, when Thomas's poems appeared they seemed superficially so like those of his mentor that some readers made the mistake of regarding them as, if not imitations, verses influenced so strongly as to bear the imprint of another man's literary personality. The debt we owe to Frost is great: had he not been able to persuade Thomas of his true vocation it is more than likely that we would have been wholly deprived of the Englishman's poems. But these poems are in no way derivative and each one is informed by the unmistakable mind and temper of its creator, reflecting a personality very different from that of the American poet.

Technically, too, the differences between the two writers are far more marked than their surface similarities. When, in 1913, Thomas reviewed the then unknown Robert Frost's *North of Boston* he wrote:

These poems are revolutionary because they lack the exaggeration of rhetoric, and even at first sight appear to lack the poetic intensity of which rhetoric is an imitation. Their language is free from the poetical words and forms that are the chief material of secondary poets . . . Yet almost all these poems are beautiful . . . Many, if not most, of the separate lines and separate sentences are plain, and, in themselves, nothing. But they are bound together and made elements of beauty by a calm eagerness of emotion . . . It is poetry because it is better than prose.

These words could justly be applied to Edward Thomas's own poetry; and his broad aims of simplicity of diction, a resolute refusal to inflate the currency of emotion, a sober regard for truth, a Coleridgean awareness of the interdependence and harmony of each element in the legitimate poem, 'the parts of which mutually support and explain each other', are also the qualities which he recognized and admired in Frost's verse; but the actual texture of their writing, the rhythm and tone, the means by which each achieved his ends, are only tangentially related.

This should become clear if we take a poem by each and place them side by side. The poems I have chosen both bear the same title, 'October':

> O hushed October morning mild,
> Thy leaves have ripened to the fall;
> Tomorrow's wind, if it be wild,
> Should waste them all.
> The crows above the forest call;
> Tomorrow they may form and go.
> O hushed October morning mild,
> Begin the hours of this day slow.
> May the day seem to us less brief.
> Hearts not averse to being beguiled,
> Beguile us in the way you know.
> Release one leaf at break of day;
> At noon release another leaf;
> One from our trees, one far away.
> Retard the sun with gentle mist;
> Enchant the land with amethyst.
> Slow, slow.
> For the grapes' sake, if they were all,
> Whose leaves are already burnt with frost,
> Whose clustered fruit must else be lost—
> For the grapes' sake along the wall.

(Robert Frost)

> The green elm with the one great bough of gold
> Lets leaves into the grass slip, one by one,—
> The short hill grass, the mushrooms small, milk-white,
> Harebell and scabious and tormentil,
> That blackberry and gorse, in dew and sun,
> Bow down to; and the wind travels too light
> To shake the fallen birch leaves from the fern;
> The gossamers wander at their own will.
> At heavier steps than birds' the squirrels scold.

The rich scene has grown fresh again and new
As spring and to the touch is not more cool
Than it is warm to the gaze; and now I might
As happy be as earth is beautiful,
Were I some other or with earth could turn
In alternation of violet and rose,
Harebell and snowdrop, at their season due,
And gorse that has no time not to be gay.
But if this be not happiness,—who knows?
Some day I shall think this a happy day,
And this mood by the name of melancholy
Shall no more blackened and obscurèd be.

                              (Edward Thomas)

The movement of Frost's verse is smoother, less hesitant, less exploratory, and the thoughtful, colloquial tone more readily lifts to a conventional lyrical voice. The feeling of transience and mortality is there, but it is generalized, not raw and personal as it is in the Thomas 'October', where the selection of natural detail presents an objective world which is, at the same time, indifferent to and yet a reversed image of the poet's private mood of melancholy which has, at its centre, a paradoxical seed of possible joy.

In general Frost is a more anecdotal poet and, in his meditative lyrics, more reticent; he is much less introspective than Thomas and all his work is coloured by his robust puritan attitudes; he is a cautious optimist, wise, ironic, and essentially God-fearing. In his poem, 'Bereft', he describes the minatory roar of an autumn gale as night approaches, and then he ends like this:

            Something sinister in the tone
            Told me my secret must be known:
            Word I was in my house alone
            Somehow must have gotten abroad,
            Word I was in my life alone,
            Word I had no one left but God.

Edward Thomas might have written a very similar poem but with one important difference; the last line would have had no place in it. When Thomas relates the events in a poem to a wider context of experience, no edifying or consolatory message appears. His mind is dark and brooding, and running through his poems is a deep nostalgia for an idealized personal and historical past which, in Christian terms, would be interpreted as the desolation consequent upon the sense of separation from God. To him happiness is always elusive: it cannot by its nature and by the nature of man be recognized at the time of its visitation but only in distant retrospect when, paradoxically, the sense of loss and the imaginative re-creation of the experience which engendered the happiness induce a condition which is part sadness and part joy.

> Then
> As now that la-la-la-! was bodiless sweet:
> Sad more than joyful it was, if I must say
> That it was one or other . . .
>   ('The Unknown Bird')

The chronic melancholy, which verged on the pathological, was the source of much of Thomas's poetry, and he was well aware of this and valued the fruitful anguish without which he would have been a more contented man but less of a poet.

IV

Much stress has so far been put on the sombre temper of Edward Thomas's character, on his self-mistrust, his melancholia, and his aching sense of mortality and the elusiveness of spiritual ease, and, while it is true that many of his poems are concerned with the evanescent nature of human happiness, and that the bright images gleam in the shadow of his brooding preoccupation with impermanence and mortality, it should be emphasized that the poetry itself is not morbid: it is often sharpened by a mordant wit, an astringent irony, and, at times, it is illumined by a real gaiety. No true work of art is monochrome, and all Edward Thomas's poems show a deliberate and fruitful opposing of contrasting moods and attitudes and a counterpoising and reconciling of the language in which these attitudes are embodied. They reflect the ceaseless inner conflict and the struggle for peace which never seemed to give him respite. Here is a rather slight poem, 'Interval', that shows clearly the way in which Thomas used opposites to create associative tensions which move gradually towards the final reconciliation of 'This roaring peace', the calm which is actually a suspended violence, the only tranquillity which the poet had experienced:

Gone the wild day:
A wilder night
Coming makes way
For brief twilight.

Where the firm soaked road
Mounts and is lost
In the high beech-wood
It shines almost.

The beeches keep
A stormy rest,
Breathing deep
Of wind from the west.

The wood is black,
With a misty steam.
Above, the cloud pack
Breaks for one gleam.

But the woodman's cot
By the ivied trees
Awakens not
To light or breeze.

It smokes aloft
Unwavering:
It hunches soft
Under storm's wing.

It has no care
For gleam or gloom:
It stays there
While I shall roam,

Die, and forget
The hill of trees,
The gleam, the wet,
This roaring peace.

In the first quatrain the stretched assonances and rhymes of *wild*, *wilder*, *night* and *twilight* hint at the opening of the space which allows the entrance of the twilit period before the stormy night. Then, in the third verse, comes the characteristic conflict between epithet and noun, the *rest* which is *stormy*, not a true and lasting stillness but a tethered anger; then come the contrasts of the black wood and the gleam as the clouds part and, later, *gleam* is first contrasted with its dark morpheme, *gloom*, and then is identified with, almost transmuted into, *wet* before the ominous paradox of the last line. In this poem, as in so many of Edward Thomas's, the symbolic landscape and objects are not contrived; they never lose their objective concreteness: the road, the beech-wood and the cottage are actual things, and if one realizes that they are also images of the harmony of created things and the indifference of nature to the condition of man whose vision is distorted and fragmentary, the freshness and precision of the description are not impaired.

In the little poem, 'Digging', (incidentally, the second of the two poems with the same title in *The Collected Poems*), one finds again the juxtaposition and final reconciliation of contrasting experiences, the sour and the sweet, sadness and mirth along with splendid evocations of touch and smell and taste:

Today I think
Only with scents,—scents dead leaves yield,
And bracken, and wild carrot's seed,
And the square mustard field;

Odours that rise
When the spade wounds the root of tree,
Rose, currant, raspberry, or goutweed,
Rhubarb or celery;

The smoke's smell, too,
Flowing from where a bonfire burns
The dead, the waste, the dangerous,
And all to sweetness turns.

It is enough
To smell, to crumble the dark earth,
While the robin sings over again
Sad songs of Autumn mirth.

Another poem called 'The Owl', which is often included in anthologies, is a simple and moving statement and, besides displaying the familiar dichromatic tensions of cold and warmth, melancholy and joy, in the linking and opposing of concrete words such as *food*, *fire*, *cold* and *tired*, Thomas uses a single word which, in the context, carries a double load of rational and emotive significance with a consequent gain in compression and impact. The poet has been out all day walking and, almost exhausted, he arrives at a country inn:

Then at the inn I had food, fire, and rest,
Knowing how hungry, cold, and tired was I.
All of the night was quite barred out except
An owl's cry, a most melancholy cry

Shaken out long and clear upon the hill,
No merry note, nor cause of merriment,
But one telling me plain what I escaped
And others could not, that night, as in I went.

And salted was my food, and my repose,
Salted and sobered, too, by the bird's voice
Speaking for all who lay under the stars,
Soldiers and poor, unable to rejoice.

It is the repeated word, *salted*, which is at once ambiguous yet absolutely right for his purposes. The owl grieves, lonely in the cold night, and the poet pities those who don't share the warmth and comfort that he is privileged to enjoy; but he is too honest to deny that, while his sympathy for the 'soldiers and poor' is authentic, his awareness of their privation adds to his own pleasure and contentment while at the same time it awakens the sense of guilt. So when he says, 'And salted was my food, and my repose', the word *salted* certainly means *flavoured* or *spiced*, but at the same time less comfortable connotations are invoked: the harshness of salt, the salt in the wound, the taste of bitterness, and of tears.

This resolute truthfulness is a characteristic of most of Edward Thomas's poetry, and the great love he felt for England is never sentimentalized, neither is it an abstract, ideological attitude nor the blind patriotic fervour that was not uncommon even among intelligent Englishmen at the time of the first World War. He loved the physical body of England; he loved her moods, seasons, hills, flowers, trees, animals and birds. Eleanor Farjeon, in *Edward Thomas: The Last Four Years*, says that she asked him during the war if he knew what he was fighting for:

He stopped, and picked up a pinch of earth. 'Literally, for this.' He crumbled it between finger and thumb, and let it fall.

His war poem, 'This Is No Case Of Petty Right Or Wrong', was one which he did not wish to preserve, no doubt considering it an occasional piece, relevant only to its historical time and situation, but, though some of the lines betray an unusual slackness of rhythm and carelessness of diction, it has in its better parts a fine laconic honesty:

> I hate not Germans, nor grow hot
> With love of Englishmen, to please newspapers.
> Beside my hate for one fat patriot
> My hatred of the Kaiser is love true:—
> A kind of god he is, banging a gong.

And the poem ends with a thoughtful, almost resigned statement of patriotism that is far more moving than any big rhetorical gesture could be, and which surely makes articulate the feelings of all men who have borne arms in defence of their country:

> The ages made her that made us from the dust:
> She is all we know and live by, and we trust
> She is good and must endure, loving her so:
> And as we love ourselves we hate her foe.

This unflinching emotional honesty also distinguishes Thomas's personal poems, in particular the one to his wife, Helen, and the poem which is entitled simply P.H.T., the initials of his father. These verses to his father are almost gratuitously cruel in their frankness and uncompromising refusal to modify in any way the inflexible hostility that the thought of his father arouses in him; but in the poem to his wife, 'No One So Much As You', the same unsentimental truthfulness produces a note of sad perplexity, of brooding tenderness. Again there is ambiguity at the heart of the poem which is a statement of love and at the same time a lament for the poet's incapacity for loving. The language throughout is unadorned and the poignant image in the last two lines flares passionately at the end of the thin, sombre fuse of contemplation. The poem ends like this:

> For I at most accept
> Your love, regretting
> That is all: I have kept
> Only a fretting
>
> That I could not return
> All that you gave
> And could not ever burn
> With the love you have,
>
> Till sometimes it did seem
> Better it were
> Never to see you more
> Than linger here
>
> With only gratitude
> Instead of love—
> A pine in solitude
> Cradling a dove.

The pine, tall, insensate, lonely and cold sustains the warm palpitating thing, but it is not warmed by the dove; as the tree gives involuntary hospitality to the nesting bird so Thomas believed that he accepted the love of his wife. The poem is as humble as it is truthful and its truth is not limited to the personal situation from which it emerges.

V

In the available biographical writings on Edward Thomas the nature of his self-divided and melancholy temperament has been examined only in a most superficial way: the accounts of the poet by his wife and by Eleanor Farjeon are delightfully myopic and from them the man emerges as scarcely more substantial than the photographs used to illustrate *Edward Thomas: The Last Four Years*, those portraits which show incarnations of the popular romantic notion of a poet, lean, sensitive, handsome and dreaming. From his writings alone one can easily see that none of his biographers has so far ventured deeply into the dark complexities of his character.

As we have seen, he felt no love for his father nor for his brothers; from his letters, it is plain that any filial feeling that he experienced was directed towards his mother. In 'No One So Much As You', he says quite explicity that he is unable properly to return his wife's love, and, while he was obviously very fond of Eleanor Farjeon, he just as obviously did not love her in the way that she loved him. He was unable to find a reason for existence in a passionate, reciprocal relationship with a woman, and he was a man wholly without belief in a religious or political panacea for the sufferings and frustrations of human life. He saw the proliferating cells of industrial civilization threatening to destroy the fair body of the land he loved. Yet he continued to search restlessly for a peace and fulfilment in which his sceptical and pessimistic intelligence could not believe.

The figure of the traveller, the lonely seeker, and the motif of the questing journey, the search for an imperfectly envisaged lost happiness which will never again be found, can be seen occurring again and again in his prose and in his poetry; but in the poems, which are so much more sharply focused than the prose meditations, it becomes clear that there is another, more personal preoccupation symbolized by his image of the Search: the lonely quest is no longer a dramatization of romantic despair, it is a psychological reality, a search for his own identity, for the reconciliation of the divided self, and his Nirvana becomes the healing peace which such a reconciliation would effect. Of course, one of the most familiar ways for the romantic poet to resolve his struggle with the problems of love and death is to direct the first against the second, to make of death his true love and to find ultimate peace only in consummation. As we saw in the poem, 'Rain', Thomas was led towards just this resolution, yet, in other poems, although the shadow of death is rarely absent, a healthy relish of the good gifts of nature and a rueful sense of irony prevent its domination.

In the rather slight but attractive poem, 'Early One Morning', Thomas begins jauntily enough:

> Early one morning in May I set out
> And nobody I knew was about.
> > I'm bound away for ever,
> > Away somewhere, away for ever.
>
> There was no wind to trouble the weathercocks.
> I had burnt my letters and darned my socks.

Then, still quite gaily, he continues:

> No one knew I was going away,
> I thought myself I should come back some day.

In the second line of this couplet there is just the slightest minatory note. Then the poem goes on:

> I heard the brook through the town gardens run.
> O sweet was the mud turned to dust by the sun.

A gate banged in a fence and banged in my head.
'A fine morning, sir', a shepherd said.

I could not return from my liberty,
To my youth and my love and my misery.

The past is the only dead thing that smells sweet,
The only sweet thing that is not also fleet.
　　I'm bound away for ever,
　　Away somewhere, away for ever.

Again in the third couplet a sombre undertone creeps in. There is the solid physical image of the mud turned to dust, but there is the sense of something else happening: mud is a life-breeding substance; dust is sterile, redolent of death. Next, the banging of the gate would seem innocent enough were it not that it banged, too, in the narrator's head. There is a hint of warning here that lends a mocking, even slightly sinister note to the shepherd's greeting. In the next two lines there is a teasing ambiguity: 'I could not return . . .' could mean 'I would hate to return; nothing would persuade me'. But linked to 'liberty' it is impossible to ignore its irony. He is not free to return.

The last four lines make it plain that the poem is not the jolly away-from-it-all piece of Georgian nonsense that the first six lines appeared to promise. Lasting happiness can be experienced only in retrospect and then it is haunted by the sense of loss. Liberty, the freedom to make choices, is an illusion. The poet says again: 'I'm bound away for ever' but by now 'bound' could mean tied, held prisoner in the continuous present, the end of which will be oblivion.

The images of the search for the unattainable are scattered through the poems, and often Thomas writes a simple description of some remembered scene such as 'The Path' which can be enjoyed for its exact observation of detail whether or not one realizes that it is also an unemphatic symbol of the poet's obsessive and always abortive quest. 'The Path' ends like this:

> But the road is houseless, and leads not to school.
> To see a child is rare there, and the eye
> Has but the road, the wood that overhangs
> And underyawns it, and the path that looks
> As if it led on to some legendary
> Or fancied place where men have wished to go
> And stay; till, sudden, it ends where the wood ends.

The finality of that last clause is total and immensely effective.

One of the most interesting of the quest poems (and in many ways one of the most interesting works in the *Collected Poems*) is 'The Other', in which the inner conflict which was central to Thomas's doubting, lonely personality is objectivized quite unequivocally. The poem is a narrative allegory told in skilfully controlled ten line stanzas: the narrator is travelling through the countryside when he comes to an inn where he is asked if he had not been there on the previous day. He realizes that, moving just ahead of him is 'The Other', a man so like himself that strangers cannot distinguish between them. He feels a nameless fear, but he is determined to pursue his other self, though he is uncertain as to what he will do if he catches his quarry. In lonely inns he asks if the mysterious Other has been seen and in one he is told that someone who might be the person he seeks has been there. When he tries to find out what kind of man his double is he learns only that the man looks like himself and is more agreeable to the locals in the inn. A girl is suspicious of him and will not answer his enquiries and he is made so angry by this encounter that he realizes that, even if he were now to meet the Other, he would be so blinded by his wrath that he would not recognize him.

There then follows a strange and rather obscure section of three stanzas where the seeker withdraws into solitude and experiences an interlude of peace before setting out again on his search. Then, at last, in the taproom of an inn he hears the Other, loudly and bitterly complaining of how he, the narrator, has made the Other's life wretched through his relentless pursuit. The narrator slips away without speaking and, hereafter, he still follows the Other, but he tries only to keep him in sight, for he is afraid of him.

The poem is a searching allegory, and it never slips into fantasy because of the poet's seriousness and because the imagery is rooted firmly in the earth and is relayed accurately through the senses. The poem begins:

> The forest ended. Glad I was
> To feel the light, and hear the hum
> Of bees, and smell the drying grass
> And the sweet mint, because I had come
> To an end of forest, and because
> Here was both road and inn, the sum
> Of what's not forest.

The forest is a real forest and the smells of the drying grass and the sweet mint can be felt in the nostrils. But we soon see that the forest is also the dark place of uncertainty from which he has emerged into a momentary and illusory sense of peace, illusory because, almost immediately, he learns of the Other who has been to the inn before him. Through a landscape that is at once concrete and symbolic he journeys, searching in crowded places and in solitude:

> I sought then in solitude.
> The wind had fallen with the night; as still
> The roads lay as the ploughland rude,
> Dark and naked, on the hill.
> Had there been ever any feud
> 'Twixt earth and sky, a mighty will
> Closed it: the crocketed dark trees,
> A dark house, dark impossible
> Cloud-towers, one star, one lamp, one peace
> Held on an everlasting lease. . . .

The obscurity of the 'solitude' stanzas is caused largely by the syntax at the end of the following lines:

> Once the name I gave to hours
> Like this was melancholy, when
> It was not happiness and powers
> Coming like exiles home again,
> And weaknesses quitting their bowers,
> Smiled and enjoyed, far off from men,
> Moments of everlastingness.
> And fortunate my search was then
> While what I sought, nevertheless,
> That I was seeking, I did not guess.

I take it that the general sense of this is that in moments of negative receptivity, when the conscious struggle towards self-discovery has been put aside, the seeker is more likely to be rewarded by illumination. The syntactical involutions of the last three lines are strange, coming from the pen of a poet who was generally so careful, but it seems likely that he did not revise them because he felt that the tortured knotted-ness was a truthful reflection of the condition he was trying to communicate. There is no such twisted complexity of meaning in the last stanza when the truth, as the poet sees it, has become clear:

> And now I dare not follow after
> Too close. I try to keep in sight,
> Dreading his frown and worse his laughter.
> I steal out of the wood to light;
> I see the swift shoot from the rafter
> By the inn door: ere I alight
> I wait and hear the starlings wheeze
> And nibble like ducks: I wait his flight.
> He goes: I follow: no release
> Until he ceases. Then I also shall cease.

So the poet has learned that the knowing self and the Other which challenges him must not meet face to face, for each is eternally hostile to the other and the judgements which each would pass on the other would be intolerable to both because they would be without charity, without love. This, I believe, is the main theme of the poem. Through the poem, Thomas understood or he reached towards an understanding of his condition. His self - contempt, his inner struggle, his inability to love were the consequences of his being unable to love himself, to extend charity towards himself. 'I am also other than what I imagine myself to be. To know this is forgiveness', wrote Simone Weil, the Christian mystic. Edward Thomas seemed to be moving towards this truth towards the end of his life.

VI

So far only the strengths of Edward Thomas's poetry have been discussed, but it would be foolish, of course, to suggest that he was a writer without fault. However, one should be careful when trying to arrive at a balanced estimate of the value of his work to distinguish between apparent weaknesses and real ones. The young reader, whose ear has been attuned to the post-Eliot idiom in English poetry, might be irritated by the quaint and quite frequent uses of 'twas, 'twill, and 'twould, which are not even needed in all cases to fit the metrical line, and he might be offended by the occasional placing of the adjective after its noun instead of in front of it, as common usage demands; these mannerisms might easily lead the young reader to believe that Thomas was working in a spent verbal tradition, whereas, in fact, few poets have shown greater resourcefulness in adapting traditional metres to the rhythms of contemporary speech, and, when one considers the period during which he was writing, his diction is remarkably free of literary influences. Those little archaisms, like certain strongly emotive nouns and epithets which are repeated insistently through the poems, and often within single poems (*Sweet, solitude, love, melancholy*), are used consciously to create a strange and individual tone, for these words are constantly working with and against a language which is as plain as good wholemeal bread.

The critic should be on his guard against being taken in by the popular heresy which began with the perfectly tenable premise that one should judge a poem by what it is rather than by what it says, but which then went on to assert that, ideally, the poem should say nothing at all, that it should be a linguistic pattern as abstract as a fugue. This heresy has made fashionable in some places a poetic diction which aims at the unpredictable and startling word or combination of words, making the verbal surprise an end in itself. The reader who approaches Edward Thomas with expectations of having a criterion of this kind satisfied will be disappointed. What his poems are depends, as all real poems depend, very much on what they say.

The real weaknesses in Thomas's work are probably the results of over-production, and quite possibly of his having spent his life as a hack writer. A few of the poems appear to have no centre of compulsion and they read like formal exercises, which is probably what they were. There are one or two others where he seems to have attempted to impose an arbitrarily chosen form on matter which simply refuses to submit, as in the poem, 'When First', where the sense units seem to bear no relation to the stanzaic pattern. Poems such as 'Health', 'March', and 'April' are spoilt by moments of whimsy, sentimentality or plain banality of thought, feeling and expression. In 'Health', for example, he writes of 'any maiden whose smile is lovelier Than sunlight upon dew'; in 'March', one is embarrassed by the schoolgirl essay image of: 'The sun filled earth and heaven with a great light And a tenderness, almost warmth, where the hail dripped, As if the mighty sun wept tears of joy.' The poem called 'April' is almost maudlin in its sentimentality, yet here one is conscious of an essential innocence of feeling that reminds one strongly of Hardy's less successful poems. Thomas's 'The Child on the Cliffs' has this innocent emotionalism and, while it is not a good poem, it is more attractive than many works of greater accomplishment and reticence.

Hardy is the English poet with whom Thomas has the most in common, and this charming little lyric, 'She Dotes', shows clearly the similarity which is sometimes a little obscured by the more colloquial idiom used by Thomas. Here the feeling is conventional enough but its music has a haunting cadence:

> She dotes on what the wild birds say
> Or hint or mock at, night and day,—
> Thrush, blackbird, all that sing in May,
> And songless plover,
> Hawk, heron, owl, and woodpecker.
> They never say a word to her
> About her lover.
>
> She laughs at them for childishness,
> She cries at them for carelessness
> Who see her going loverless
> Yet sing and chatter
> Just as when he was not a ghost,
> Nor ever ask her what she has lost
> Or what is the matter.
>
> Yet she has fancied blackbirds hide
> A secret, and that thrushes chide
> Because she thinks death can divide
> Her from her lover:
> And she has slept, trying to translate
> The word the cuckoo cries to his mate
> Over and over.

But of course this is Thomas working in a minor key, and the poem hardly justifies the rather large claims I have made for the technical strength and originality of his best work. These qualities are better shown in this little known poem, 'Over the Hills':

> Often and often it came back again
> To mind, the day I passed the horizon ridge
> To a new country, the path I had to find
> By half-gaps that were stiles once in the hedge,

The pack of scarlet clouds running across
The harvest evening that seemed endless then
And after, and the inn where all were kind,
All were strangers. I did not know my loss
Till one day twelve months later suddenly
I leaned upon my spade and saw it all,
Though far beyond the sky-line. It became
Almost a habit through the year for me
To lean and see it and think to do the same
Again for two days and a night. Recall
Was vain: no more could the restless brook
Ever turn back and climb the waterfall
To the lake that rests and stirs not in its nook,
As in the hollow of the collar-bone
Under the mountain's head of rush and stone.

The theme, that the past is omnipresent yet beyond recall, is explored in easy conversational rhythms based on the pentameter but with shifting emphases that give the movement a suitable hesitancy, a feeling of tentative reflection. The rhyme scheme is particularly interesting when one considers that the poem was written almost half a century ago: Thomas uses rhyme and, in line four, half-rhyme, very much in the way that a poet of the fifties or sixties like Philip Larkin uses it: that is to say, not in conformity with a strict, preconceived pattern, but at intervals so spaced that the chime of vowel and consonant occur faintly, uninsistently until the poem draws towards its end, when the rhymes are closer together, more emphatic before the finality of the terminating couplet. The language is plain, unadorned by imagery, until the last five lines when the fine image of the lake 'in the hollow of the collar-bone' comes with the force of a revelation.

Had he not been killed it seems likely that Thomas would have developed the narrative gifts shown in those longer and neglected narrative poems, 'Lob', 'Up In The Wind', and 'Wind And Mist'. In 'Lob', which is the gayest of his poems, with only the gentlest of nostalgic overtones, he celebrates in easily flowing rhymed couplets the robust and poetic

naming spirit that is part of the heritage of rural England, the
creator of place names such as The Hog's Back and Mother
Dunch's Buttocks; fairy stories, legends, jokes and the pet
names for wild flowers and birds. Both 'Up In The Wind'
and 'Wind And Mist' are tougher, bleaker pieces of work,
laced by sardonic humour, and both demonstrate his skill in
using the pentameter as a base for blank verse which is
neither prosy nor strained. Here is the girl in 'Up In The
Wind' who has returned from London to her birthplace in a
lonely part of England to look after the little isolated inn for
her father:

> . . . all I ever had to thank
> The wind for was for blowing the sign down.
> Time after time it blew down and I could sleep.
> At last they fixed it, and it took a thief
> To move it, and we've never had another:
> It's lying at the bottom of the pond.
> But no one's moved the wood from off the hill
> There at the back, although it makes a noise
> When the wind blows, as if a train were running
> The other side, a train that never stops
> Or ends. And the linen crackles on the line
> Like a wood fire rising.

The easy colloquial movement of this and the unforced but
striking imagery suggest that Thomas might have made a
dramatist: in his own words 'it is poetry because it is better
than prose'. But there is little to be gained by speculating on
what Edward Thomas might have done and we should be
grateful for the image he has left us of his world, that place
where melancholy and muted gaiety are inextricably mixed,
a place peopled by characters half real, half mythical, who are
never still, always passing out of the poet's orbit; a place
where a fresh wind of irony blows away the maudlin and the
false. The reader who finds that he is barred from entering
this world because of his training, prejudices, and precon-
ceptions concerning the nature of poetry would do well to
re-think the principles on which his judgements are based,

and the reader who is barred by defects of sensibility and imagination must accept the fact that he is deaf and blind to the work of one of the best of England's minor poets; though Thomas himself in his poem, 'Aspens', faced the probability of such neglect or lack of sympathy with humility and resignation:

> And it would be the same were no house near.
> Over all sorts of weather, men, and times,
> Aspens must shake their leaves and men may hear
> But need not listen, more than to my rhymes.
>
> Whatever wind blows, while they and I have leaves
> We cannot other than an aspen be
> That ceaselessly, unreasonably grieves,
> Or so men think who like a different tree.

EDWARD THOMAS

A Select Bibliography

(Place of publication London, unless stated otherwise)

Bibliography:
EDWARD THOMAS: A BIOGRAPHY AND A BIBLIOBRAPHY, by R. P. Eckert (1937).

Collected Works and Selections:
COLLECTED POEMS (1920).
COLLECTED POEMS, edited, with an appreciation by W. de la Mare (1928).
COLLECTED POEMS (1936).
SELECTED POEMS (1926).
SELECTED POEMS, edited by E. Garnett. Newtown (1927).
CHOSEN ESSAYS. Newtown (1926).
SELECTED PROSE, edited by R. Gant (1948).

Separate Works:
THE WOODLAND LIFE (1897). *Essays and a Diary*
HORAE SOLITARIAE (1902). *Essays*
OXFORD (1903). *Topography*
ROSE ACRE PAPERS (1904). *Essays*
BEAUTIFUL WALES (1905). *Topography*
THE HEART OF ENGLAND (1906). *Essay*
RICHARD JEFFERIES (1909). *Criticism*
THE SOUTH COUNTRY (1909) *Topography*
—the second edition of 1932 has an introduction by Helen Thomas, the poet's wife.
REST AND UNREST (1910). *Essays*
FEMININE INFLUENCE ON THE POETS (1910). *Criticism*
WINDSOR CASTLE (1910). *Topography*
LIGHT AND TWILIGHT (1911). *Essays*
THE ISLE OF WIGHT (1911). *Topography*
MAURICE MAETERLINCK (1911). *Criticism*
CELTIC STORIES Oxford (1911) *Fiction*
—traditional tales retold by Edward Thomas.
THE TENTH MUSE (1911). *Essays*
ALGERNON CHARLES SWINBURNE (1912). *Criticism*
LAFCADIO HEARN (1912). *Criticism*

NORSE TALES Oxford (1912). *Fiction*
—traditional tales retold by Edward Thomas.
THE ICKNIELD WAY (1913). *Topography*
THE COUNTRY (1913). *Essay*
THE HAPPY-GO-LUCKY MORGANS (1913). *Fiction*
WALTER PATER (1913). *Criticism*
THE PURSUIT OF SPRING (1914). *Topography*
LIFE OF THE DUKE OF MARLBOROUGH (1915). *Biography*
FOUR-AND-TWENTY BLACKBIRDS (1915). *Children's Stories*
SIX POEMS (1916)
—published pseudonymously as 'By Edward Eastaway'.
KEATS (1916). *Criticism*
POEMS (1917).
A LITERARY PILGRIM IN ENGLAND (1917). *Topography*
LAST POEMS (1918).
CLOUD CASTLE (1922). *Essays*
ESSAYS OF TODAY AND YESTERDAY (1926).
TWO POEMS (1927).
THE LAST SHEAF (1928). *Essays*
CHILDHOOD: A FRAGMENT OF AUTOBIOGRAPHY (1938).

Note: Edward Thomas edited a number of selections and anthologies,
for example *Some British Birds* (1908) and *George Borrow* (1912).

Some Critical and Biographical Studies:
SOME SOLDIER POETS, by T. S. Moore (1919).
MODERN BRITISH POETRY, by L. Untermeyer. New York (1920).
AS IT WAS, by H. Thomas (1926)
—a biography by the poet's wife, published with *World Without End*,
its sequel, in one volume, 1956.
WORLD WITHOUT END, by H. Thomas (1931).
NEW BEARINGS IN ENGLISH POETRY, by F. R. Leavis (1932).
THE TREND OF MODERN POETRY, by G. Bullough (1934).
EDWARD THOMAS: A BIOGRAPHY AND A BIBLIOGRAPHY, by R. F. Eckert
(1937).
TO THE MEMORY OF EDWARD THOMAS, by J. Guthrie (1937).
THE LIFE AND LETTERS OF EDWARD THOMAS, by J. Moore (1939).
'A Note on Edward Thomas', by G. Bottomley, *The Welsh Review*,
vol. IV, No. 3 (1945) pp. 166-179.

'The Poetry of Edward Thomas', by C. Day Lewis. In *Essays by Divers Hands* (Trans. Royal Soc. of Lit., vol. XXVIII) Oxford (1956)
—the Giff Edmonds Memorial Lecture.
EDWARD THOMAS, by H. Coombes (1956).
MEMOIRS, by E. Farjeon (1958)
—Book One: 'Edward Thomas: The Last Four Years.'
HARDY, DE LA MARE AND EDWARD THOMAS, by H. Coombes (vol. 7, 'The Modern Age', *Pelican Guide to English Literature* (1961).

———————

¶Works by Edward Thomas are quoted by kind permission of Mrs. Helen Thomas; our thanks are also due to Messrs. Jonathan Cape Ltd. and to Messrs. Holt, Rinehart & Winston Inc. for permission to quote from *The Complete Poems of Robert Frost*.

WRITERS AND THEIR WORK

General Editor: BONAMY DOBRÉE

The first 55 issues in the Series appeared under the General Editorship of T. O. BEACHCROFT

Sixteenth Century and Earlier:

FRANCIS BACON: J. Max Patrick
CHAUCER: Nevill Coghill
ENGLISH BIBLE: Donald Coggan
ENGLISH MARITIME WRITING:
    Hakluyt to Cook: Oliver Warner
MALORY: M. C. Bradbrook
MARLOWE: Philip Henderson
SIDNEY: Kenneth Muir
SKELTON: Peter Green
SPENSER: Rosemary Freeman
WYATT: Sergio Baldi

Seventeenth Century:

SIR THOMAS BROWNE: Peter Green
BUNYAN: Henri Talon
CAVALIER POETS: Robin Skelton
DONNE: F. Kermode
DRYDEN: Bonamy Dobrée
ENGLISH SERMONS: Arthur Pollard
HERBERT: T. S. Eliot
HERRICK: John Press
HOBBES: T. E. Jessop
BEN JONSON: J. B. Bamborough
LOCKE: Maurice Cranston
ANDREW MARVELL: John Press
MILTON: E. M. W. Tillyard
SHAKESPEARE: C. J. Sisson
  CHRONICLES: Clifford Leech
  EARLY COMEDIES: Derek Traversi
  FINAL PLAYS: F. Kermode
  HISTORIES: L. C. Knights
  LATE COMEDIES: G. K. Hunter
  PROBLEM PLAYS: Peter Ure
  ROMAN PLAYS: T. J. B. Spencer
THREE METAPHYSICAL POETS:
             Margaret Willy
IZAAK WALTON: Margaret Bottrall

Eighteenth Century:

BERKELEY: T. E. Jessop
BLAKE: Kathleen Raine
BOSWELL: P. A. W. Collins
BURKE: T. E. Utley
BURNS: David Daiches

COWPER: N. Nicholson
CRABBE: R. L. Brett
DEFOE: J. R. Sutherland
ENGLISH HYMNS: A. Pollard
FIELDING: John Butt
GIBBON: C. V. Wedgwood
GOLDSMITH: A. Norman Jeffares
GRAY: R. W. Ketton-Cremer
JOHNSON: S. C. Roberts
POPE: Ian Jack
RICHARDSON: R. F. Brissenden
SHERIDAN: W. A. Darlington
SMART: Geoffrey Grigson
SMOLLETT: Laurence Brander
STEELE, ADDISON AND THEIR
  PERIODICAL ESSAYS:
             A. R. Humphreys
STERNE: D. W. Jefferson
SWIFT: J. Middleton Murry
HORACE WALPOLE: Hugh Honour

Nineteenth Century:

MATTHEW ARNOLD: Kenneth Allott
JANE AUSTEN: S. Townsend Warner
BAGEHOT: N. St. John-Stevas
THE BRONTË SISTERS: P. Bentley
BROWNING: John Bryson
SAMUEL BUTLER: G. D. H. Cole
BYRON: Herbert Read
CARLYLE: David Gascoyne
LEWIS CARROLL: Derek Hudson
CLOUGH: Isobel Armstrong
COLERIDGE: Kathleen Raine
DICKENS: K. J. Fielding
DISRAELI: Paul Bloomfield
GEORGE ELIOT: Lettice Cooper
ENGLISH TRAVELLERS IN THE NEAR
  EAST: Robin Fedden
FITZGERALD: Joanna Richardson
MRS. GASKELL: Miriam Allott
GISSING: A. C. Ward
THOMAS HARDY: R. A. Scott-James
HAZLITT: J. B. Priestley
HOOD: Laurence Brander
G. M. HOPKINS: Geoffrey Grigson

T. H. HUXLEY: William Irvine
KEATS: Edmund Blunden
LAMB: Edmund Blunden
LANDOR: G. Rostrevor Hamilton
MACAULAY: G. R. Potter
JOHN STUART MILL: M. Cranston
WILLIAM MORRIS: P. Henderson
NEWMAN: J. M. Cameron
PATER: Iain Fletcher
PEACOCK: J. I. M. Stewart
ROSSETTI: Oswald Doughty
RUSKIN: Peter Quennell
SIR WALTER SCOTT: Ian Jack
SHELLEY: Stephen Spender
R. L. STEVENSON: G. B. Stern
SWINBURNE: H. J. C. Grierson
TENNYSON: F. L. Lucas
THACKERAY: Laurence Brander
FRANCIS THOMPSON: P. Butter
TROLLOPE: Hugh Sykes Davies
OSCAR WILDE: James Laver
WORDSWORTH: Helen Darbishire

Twentieth Century:

W. H. AUDEN: Richard Hoggart
HILAIRE BELLOC: Renée Haynes
ARNOLD BENNETT: F. Swinnerton
EDMUND BLUNDEN: Alec M. Hardie
ELIZABETH BOWEN: Jocelyn Brooke
ROBERT BRIDGES: John Sparrow
ROY CAMPBELL: David Wright
JOYCE CARY: Walter Allen
G. K. CHESTERTON: C. Hollis
WINSTON CHURCHILL: John Connell
R. G. COLLINGWOOD:
            E. W. F. Tomlin
I. COMPTON-BURNETT:
            Pamela Hansford Johnson
JOSEPH CONRAD: Oliver Warner
WALTER DE LA MARE: K. Hopkins
THE DETECTIVE STORY IN BRITAIN:
            Julian Symons
NORMAN DOUGLAS: Ian Greenlees
T. S. ELIOT: M. C. Bradbrook
ENGLISH TRANSLATORS AND
      TRANSLATIONS: J. M. Cohen

RONALD FIRBANK and JOHN
      BETJEMAN: Jocelyn Brooke
FORD MADOX FORD: Kenneth Young
E. M. FORSTER: Rex Warner
CHRISTOPHER FRY: Derek Stanford
JOHN GALSWORTHY: R. H. Mottram
ROBERT GRAVES: M. Seymour Smith
GRAHAM GREENE: Francis Wyndham
L. P. HARTLEY and ANTHONY POW-
      ELL: P. Bloomfield and B. Bergonzi
A. E. HOUSMAN: Ian Scott-Kilvert
ALDOUS HUXLEY: Jocelyn Brooke
HENRY JAMES: Michael Swan
JAMES JOYCE: J. I. M. Stewart
RUDYARD KIPLING: B. Dobrée
D. H. LAWRENCE: Kenneth Young
C. DAY LEWIS: Clifford Dyment
WYNDHAM LEWIS: E. W. F. Tomlin
KATHERINE MANSFIELD: Ian Gordon
JOHN MASEFIELD: L. A. G. Strong
SOMERSET MAUGHAM: J. Brophy
EDWIN MUIR: J. C. Hall
J. MIDDLETON MURRY: Philip Mairet
GEORGE ORWELL: Tom Hopkinson
POETS OF 1939-45 WAR:
            R. N. Currey
THE POWYS BROTHERS:
            R. C. Churchill
J. B. PRIESTLEY: Ivor Brown
HERBERT READ: Francis Berry
BERTRAND RUSSELL: Alan Dorward
BERNARD SHAW: A. C. Ward
EDITH SITWELL: John Lehmann
OSBERT SITWELL: Roger Fulford
C. P. SNOW: William Cooper
STRACHEY: R. A. Scott-James
J. M. SYNGE and LADY GREGORY:
            Elizabeth Coxhead
DYLAN THOMAS: G. S. Fraser
G. M. TREVELYAN: J. H. Plumb
WAR POETS: 1914-18: E. Blunden
EVELYN WAUGH: Christopher Hollis
H. G. WELLS: Montgomery Belgion
CHARLES WILLIAMS: J. Heath-Stubbs
VIRGINIA WOOLF:
            Bernard Blackstone
W. B. YEATS: G. S. Fraser